The
Essential
RuPaul

The Essential RuPaul

HERSTORY, PHILOSOPHY & HER FIERCEST QUEENS

John Davis
ILLUSTRATIONS by LIBBY VANDERPLOEG

Smith Street Books

Contents

*HER*story

"Once upon a time there was a little black boy born and raised in San Diego, California, who at fifteen moved to Atlanta to study Performance Art and then went on to become the most famous supermodel in the world."

RuPaul Andre Charles was a boy who always liked to play with all of the colours from the crayon box. Affirmed by his mother from an early age that he was going to be a star, RuPaul was given his unique first name by her because "ain't another motherf*cker alive with a name like that". After moving out of home to pursue a career in the entertainment industry studying at the North Atlanta School of Performing Arts in his teens, Ru soon dropped out knowing he needed to find his calling – something that would utilise his effervescent personality and incomparable charm.

A Jack of all trades from the outset, RuPaul of the early 1980s led a punk rock band called Wee Wee Pole, go-go danced on bars, presented a cable access political gay talk show and hosted numerous local events as a smeared-lipstick, combat-boot-wearing, anti-establishment type of performer. Once the Atlanta scene grew tired for RuPaul, he moved to New York City chasing his own star on the rise with other Atlanta nightlife notables Larry Tee and Lady Bunny. Teaming up with his hometown club family in New York, RuPaul began creating the original Starrbooty series, a pastiche of 1960s blaxploitation films, which were distributed in the nightclubs he performed in, before discovering that his dreams of superstardom in the Big Apple were harder to reach than anticipated. After struggling for the best part of the 80s and his several moves from couch to couch and back across the country to live with his sister, Ru resettled in New York in 1989 determined to change up his act to become RuPaul the glamazon.

Following his crowning as the Queen of Manhattan and a guest appearance in The B-52s music video for "Love Shack", RuPaul swiftly changed gears and began his ascendancy by signing with record label Tommy Boy and recording his debut studio album *Supermodel of the World*. The lead single "Supermodel (You Better Work)" was released in November 1992 and became a hit in the US and across Europe making RuPaul, the 6'7" man in drag, a household name. In the years following RuPaul hosted the MTV Video Music Awards and the Brit Awards (with Sir Elton John) and released a UK #7 hit single with Sir Elton – a cover of the seventies hit "Don't Go Breaking My Heart" produced by disco legend Giorgio Moroder. Modelling contracts with makeup giant M.A.C. Cosmetics and a book release (*Lettin' It All Hang Out* in 1995) kept Ru's star on the rise throughout the mid 1990s before he began hosting his own talk show, *The RuPaul Show*, with radio hostess Michelle Visage in 1996. A melting pot of A-list celebrity interviews, live performances and even political discussions, *The RuPaul Show* ran for 100 episodes over two seasons and allowed Ru to meet and perform alongside many of his childhood idols including Cher and Diana Ross. Finishing off the decade with a guest starring role in *The Brady Bunch* remake film and a legendary duet of "It's Raining Men" with another of his idols, Martha Wash, RuPaul was about to embark on the third phase of his drag career – going underground again.

Faced with the post-9/11 Republican world at his doorstep, RuPaul made the creative and professional decision to take a break from showbiz after what was an incredibly successful run. Quietly releasing studio and remix albums as well as the odd club single between 2004 and 2008, RuPaul, the "Supermodel of the World" was faced with a lack of promotion and support from the industry that built him up only ten years prior. Armed with a new outlook on his place in the universe, RuPaul began working on a new television opportunity, inspired by the success of Tyra Banks' *America's Next Top Model*.

RuPaul's Drag Race aired its first season in 2009 on LGBT-focused lifestyle cable channel Logo TV and the rest is *her*story. Going from strength to strength over seven main cycles and one *All Stars* season between 2009 and 2015, *Drag Race* harnessed the revisiting of 1990s pop culture in mainstream society. Bringing together fierce drag competitors from across the US, Puerto Rico and even Australia to a gauntlet where sewing, performance, styling and comedy skills are tested to discover "America's Next Drag Superstar", RuPaul has created a whole new world of drag aspiration. Incorporation of new RuPaul dance anthems like "Glamazon", "Sissy That Walk" and "Cover Girl" into the programming allowed for new fans of his music to jump on board the train that started two decades earlier. As the popularity of the show and viewership increased from season to season RuPaul created RuPaul's DragCon in 2015, the first ever convention focused on drag queens, their artistry and cultural impact. RuPaul, the ultimate glamazon, supermodel and all round queen bee isn't showing signs of slowing down... and neither are his girls.

RuFacts

THE MUSIC

SELECTED DISCOG-RU-PHY:
RuPaul is Star Booty: Original Motion Picture Soundtrack (1986)

Supermodel of the World (1993)

Foxy Lady (1996)

Ho, Ho, Ho (1997)

RuPaul Red Hot (2004)

Starrbooty: Original Motion Picture Soundtrack (2007)

Champion (2009)

Glamazon (2011)

Born Naked (2014)

Realness (2015)

Greatest Hits (2015)

Slay Belles (2015)

SASSIEST SINGLES:
"Supermodel (You Better Work)" (1992)

"A Shade Shady (Now Prance)" (1993)

"Don't Go Breaking My Heart" (with Elton John) (1993)

"Looking Good, Feeling Gorgeous" (2004)

"Cover Girl" (2009)

"Peanut Butter" (featuring Big Freedia) (2012)

"Sissy That Walk" (2014)

THE MOGUL

RU-ENTERPRISE MERCHANDISE:
RuPaul Limited Edition Collector's Figurine

"Glamazon" fragrance by Colorevolution

RuPaul Bar (peanut butter and sea salt chocolate bar) from Sweet! candy store, Hollywood

Lettin' It All Hang Out (biography)

Workin' It: RuPaul's Guide to Life, Liberty and the Pursuit of Style (self help guide)

WHICH RU ARE YOU?:
RuPaul as Mrs. Cummings (*The Brady Bunch Movie*, 1995)

RuPaul as Rachel Tensions (*To Wong Foo, Thanks for Everything! Julie Newmar*, 1995)

RuPaul as Starrbooty (*Starrbooty*, 2007)

RuPaul as Tyrell Tyrelle (*Another Gay Sequel: Gays Gone Wild*, 2008)

RuPaul as Rudolph (*Ugly Betty*, 2010)

THE ICON

RU'S ICONIC LOOKS:
Confederate Flag Dress by
Marlene Stewart, as seen
in *To Wong Foo, Thanks for
Everything! Julie Newmar*

Isis Winged Showgirl by Bob
Mackie, as seen at the 1995
VH1 Fashion and Music Awards

Golden Glamazon by Zaldy,
as seen in *RuPaul's Drag Race*
Season 4 promo

Supermodel of the World by
Zaldy, as seen in the music
video for "Supermodel
(You Better Work)"

SIGNATURE LOOK:
Supermodel of the World
Realness

TYPE:
The Glamazon

Michelle Visage

"Stop relying on that body!"

DRAG RACE JUDGE:

Seasons 3–7, including *All Stars* Season 1

CLAIMS TO FAME:

Member of 90s R&B girl group Seduction who released hit single "Two to Make it Right"

Co-hosted *The RuPaul Show* on VH1 from 1996

Contestant on Season 15 of UK *Celebrity Big Brother* (5th place)

MICHELLE'S ETERNAL QUEENS:

Bianca Del Rio – "She is the epitome of a drag queen, quite typical in NYC, actually. Bianca to me is the very crux of what I think of when I think of drag. Tons of heavily applied makeup, loud mouthed, dirty, funny and always making me laugh – and that's not easy."

Raven – "Raven is a fierce, fierce, fierce queen who is funny. Personality just heightens your drag. When you're up there you can be the most gorgeous thing I've ever seen, but if you don't have the personality to back it up, I'm bored."

Alaska – "That's my baby... Alaska and I got really close during *Rocky* (*Horror Picture Show*) and I helped her through her sobriety. I feel very blessed and lucky to spend that time with Alaska. She's blossomed into this super talent that I always knew she was."

Manila Luzon – "I was accused of loving her most in Season 3. Manila was the apple of my eye. Again with the creativity and the camp, even though Manila's gorgeous and she could do pageantry, she does this kind of camp pageantry. I look forward to the outfits she brings."

Detox – "One of my favourite queens on the face of the earth. If I could marry Detox I would. I have such a special bond with Matthew and she has the softest lips on the earth."

Santino Rice

"Your mother lied to you — you're really not talented!"

DRAG RACE JUDGE:

Seasons 1–6, including *All Stars* Season 1

CLAIMS TO FAME:

Contestant on Season 2 of *Project Runway* (3rd place)

Judge of the Miss Universe 2006 pageant

Starred in the Lifetime reality show *On the Road with Austin and Santino* (2010)

SHADIEST RUNWAY CRITIQUES:

Ongina – "A woman in a pantsuit is really great. A drag queen in a pant suit... and not tucking, is a man."

Pandora Boxx – "If you're wearing this to look glamorous it's not working for me. If you're gonna look like a coke whore take the joke even further."

Shangela – "As far as her fashion sense... her style... she's clueless."

Latrice Royale – "This gown that you came out in it's like ugh... it's so heavy. It looks like a couch from Rent-A-Center."

Alyssa Edwards – "That dress is probably one of the worst dresses I've ever seen on this runway in five seasons. It's such a mess. I don't get what it's supposed to be."

Kelly Mantle – "Nothing says high fashion like white polyester. That skirt is horrible. Horrible."

Adore Delano

"I'm not polished enough?
I'm polish remover, b*tch!"

WHAT'S THE T?

A seasoned reality TV competitor, Danny Noriega made it as far as the semi finals on the seventh season of *American Idol* in 2008 before unleashing persona Adore Delano, his YouTube drag character, in 2009. Adore was the perfect blend of Noriega's fiery pop rock sensibility and his mother's so called "ex-chola" attitude. In the lead up to her appearance on *RuPaul's Drag Race* in 2014 Adore, inspired by hostess and *Drag Race* royalty Raven, competed and won her first drag contest at Micky's in West Hollywood in 2011.

Competing in the *Race* was a challenge for the green Delano, who fought hard to shake off the criticisms of her sloppy performance and aesthetic. She triumphed in "Shade: The Rusical" and the "Oh No She Betta Don't" rap challenge as well as in the fragrance advertisement challenge alongside drag sister Laganja Estranja harnessing her personality and charm to forward her way into the top three of the contest. Although finishing as a co-runner up with Courtney Act, Adore won the hearts of the *Drag Race* audience and took control of the second phase of her plan to take over the world.

Releasing her debut album *Till Death Do Us Party* soon after the conclusion of Season 6, Adore Delano went on tour to promote the album across the world. Truly a cross-over star, Delano's album charted higher than any other contestant's releases on the American charts and she has created numerous music videos for the singles, including "I Look F*ckin' Cool" starring Alaska and Nina Flowers.

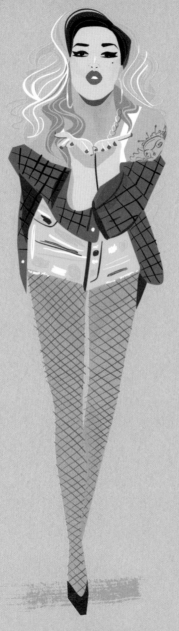

QUICK STATS

DRAG RACE:
Season 6

RANKING:
Co-runner Up

POST DRAG RACE:
Released debut album *Till Death Do Us Party* (charted at #59 on the US *Billboard* 200 chart); starred in Starbucks' first LGBT advertisement with Bianca Del Rio

SIGNATURE LOOK:
Band T-shirt and Combat Boots Realness

TYPE:
The Diamond in the Rough

FAN-FAVOURITE PERFORMANCE:
"Patron Tequila"
by Paradiso Girls

Alaska

"Hieeeeeee!"

WHAT'S THE T?

Alaska Thunderf*ck 5000 (Justin Honard) cut his teeth as a drag queen in 2009 at Fubar in West Hollywood after a departure from acting. Hailing from Pittsburgh, Alaska returned to her hometown in 2010 to pursue both a drag career and relationship with Sharon Needles with whom she formed the band Haus of Haunt. Inspired by tranimal and other non-conformist styles of drag, Alaska was the perfect blend of trash and glamour and drew the attention of fans for many years prior to her appearance on *Drag Race*.

Following the win of then-partner Sharon Needles, Alaska powered through Season 5 of the *Race* notoriously never having to lip-synch for her life just like Season 2 winner Tyra Sanchez. Winning the "Sugar Ball" and "Scent of a Drag Queen" challenges late in the contest solidified Thunderf*ck's brand of trash-glamour as well as her raunchy sense of humour that garnered such wide adoration from viewers of the competition; fans were tickled pink by her "Red for Filth". Although she came co-runner up with Florida powerhouse Roxxxy Andrews to Jinkx Monsoon, Alaska Thunderf*ck was able to shake off the label of "Sharon's Boyfriend" and began the road to becoming what Willam has described as "The Future of Drag".

Following the *Race* with stage performances in *The Rocky Horror Show*, *Sex and the City*, cabaret show *Red for Filth* and a Stevie Nicks tribute called *Stevie Forever*, Alaska became a recording artist. In conjunction with being a spokesmodel in an American Apparel advertisement, she released music with fellow "AAA Girls" Willam and Courtney Act and toured her debut album *Anus* across the globe in 2015.

DRAG RACE:
Season 5

RANKING:
Co-runner Up

POST DRAG RACE:
Stars in weekly World of Wonder
produced web series *Bro'Laska*
with her brother Cory Binney;
spokesmodel for American
Apparel in 2014 alongside
Willam and Courtney Act;
released debut album *Anus*
(2015) featuring the singles
"Hieee" and "This Is My Hair".

SIGNATURE LOOK:
Tacky Blonde Bombshell
Realness

TYPE:
The Trash to Treasure Queen

FAN-FAVOURITE PERFORMANCE:
"How Many Licks?" by Lil' Kim

Alyssa Edwards

"Every woman has a secret. Mine happens to be a little bigger."

WHAT'S THE T?

A long-time competitor in the drag pageantry circuit, Justin Johnson as Alyssa Edwards competed and won numerous pageant titles including Miss Gay Texas America 2004–2005, Miss Gay UsofA 2006 and All American Goddess 2010. A dancing queen and fierce performer from Mesquite, Texas, Alyssa appeared in the 2008 documentary *Pageant* and built her Beyond Belief Dance Company prior to her appearance on *RuPaul's Drag Race*.

Emerging as one of the most well rounded performance queens in *Drag Race* herstory, Alyssa Edwards was immediately positioned as the nemesis of fellow contest Coco Montrese with whom they shared the history of pageant dethroning and title stripping. The history of these two contestants reared its head throughout Season 5, culminating in an epic Lip-synch for Your Life to Paula Abdul's "Cold Hearted Snake" where Edwards was ultimately out-performed by her pageant sister. Prior to her elimination Alyssa became one hell of a quotable queen melding her southern charm with old school catchphrases to create memorable lines such as "backrolls!?", "get a grip, get a life and get over it" and "I don't get cute, I get drop dead gorgeous".

Winning a new legion of fans from the show Alyssa has gone on to star in her own web series *Alyssa's Secret* where she talks about a range of topics from wigs and nails to dating in drag. As a fashionista Edwards has graced the LA Fashion Week MarcoMarco runway for three years. She is currently working on producing her own reality television series based on her dance company.

QUICK STATS

DRAG RACE:
Season 5

RANKING:
6th place

POST DRAG RACE:
Stars in her very own World
of Wonder web series *Alyssa's
Secret*; continues to direct her
Texas-based dance company
Beyond Belief; choreographed
and performed with pop star
Miley Cyrus at the 2015 MTV
Video Music Awards

SIGNATURE LOOK:
Miss America Realness

TYPE:
The Dancing Queen

FAN-FAVOURITE PERFORMANCE:
"Indestructible Medley"
by Various Artists

BeBe Zahara Benet

"Face. Face. Face. I give face, beauty, face."

WHAT'S THE T?

Hailing from Cameroon, Nea Marshall Kudi worked as a male model in Paris and had his first taste of drag after filling in for an unexpected no-show of a female model. BeBe Zahara Benet was born out of the gender-bending runway moment a "strong and c*nty character illusion created for entertainment and the artistic expression of the feminine psyche".

Emerging from the Minneapolis drag scene BeBe starred in the very first season of *RuPaul's Drag Race* bringing a sense of international influence and worldly aesthetic to the competition. Winning two main challenges she was one of the strongest competitors only having to lip-synch for her life in a wig-throwing showdown against Ongina to Britney Spears' "Stronger". Always poised, softly spoken and serving face, BeBe Zahara Benet snatched the crown from runners up Nina Flowers and Rebecca Glasscock after an iconic appearance in the first *Drag Race* music video for "Cover Girl".

After her triumphant win in the first season of *Drag Race* BeBe went on to create a theatre piece called *Queendom* where she incorporated live original music that fused pop music with African rhythms, elaborate costuming, live singers and dance elements. In addition to her regular club spots BeBe chose to take on the challenge of public speaking at American universities discussing how her West African upbringing balances with her drag persona and life as a gay man.

QUICK STATS

DRAG RACE:
Season 1

RANKING:
Winner

POST DRAG RACE:
Released several dance singles
on iTunes including "I'm the
Sh*t" (2009), "Cameroon" (2010)
and "Face" (2014); Fierce Drag
Professor at *RuPaul's Drag U*;
makes appearances across the
United States as a public speaker
on pride, drag and the affect of
her West African upbringing

SIGNATURE LOOK:
African Animal Skin Realness

TYPE:
The Cameroonian Goddess

FAN-FAVOURITE PERFORMANCE:
"Miss US of A 2005 Medley"
by Various Artists

with
HAIR,
HEELS
and
ATTITUDE
HONEY,
I am through the roof

BenDeLaCreme

"DeLa for short. De for shorter. Ms Creme if you're nasty."

WHAT'S THE T?

While pursuing a Bachelor of Fine Arts at the Arts Institute of Chicago, the now Seattle-based Benjamin Putnam started his drag career in 2002 as BenDeLaCreme. A terminally delightful drag queen housewife, DeLa's inherently political show sensibility reflected her upbringing within the drag king scene of Chicago. Following her move to Seattle, she ran DeLouRue Presents, a theatrical production company producing work featuring both drag and burlesque acts, notably Season 5 winner Jinkx Monsoon. Prior to her appearance on *Drag Race* DeLa also appeared on screen in documentary film *Waxie Moon* by Wes Hurley.

Miss Congeniality of the sixth season of *RuPaul's Drag Race*, BenDeLaCreme demonstrated exceptional sewing, comedic, musical and impersonation skills throughout the contest. Although winner of the fan-favourite "Snatch Game" portraying actress Maggie Smith in her role from *Downton Abbey*, DeLa fought off stiff critique from the judges that she hid behind character facades. In a *Drag Race* first, BenDeLaCreme lip synched for her life on two separate controversial occasions against Darienne Lake, ultimately missing out on making the top four of the contest.

Following her season of *Drag Race*, DeLa has continued to produce shows with DeLouRue including *Freedom Fantasia* the "liberty-encrusted, justice-soaked, apple-pie-scented pageant of patriotism". In conjunction with Atomic Cosmetics she has also curated her own line of cosmetics and fragrance.

QUICK STATS

DRAG RACE:
Season 6

RANKING:
5th place (Miss Congeniality)

POST DRAG RACE:
Performed in a reimagining of
Hocus Pocus with San Francisco
drag legend Peaches Christ and
Jinkx Monsoon; curated her own
line of cruelty-free cosmetics and
fragrance (Candy from a Baby)
with Atomic Cosmetics

SIGNATURE LOOK:
Kitsch Housewife Realness

TYPE:
The Character Queen

FAN-FAVOURITE PERFORMANCE:
"The Little Mermaid Medley"
from *The Little Mermaid
Original Soundtrack*

Bianca Del Rio

"My style is very Joan Crawford/ Bozo the Clown. It's versatile. I'm not, but the look is."

WHAT'S THE T?

Hailing from Gretna, Louisiana, Roy Haylock started his drag artistry in 1996 after working for many years as a costume designer. Emerging as Bianca Del Rio, the sharp-tongued New Orleans Gay Entertainer of the Year performed regularly before moving to New York after Hurricane Katrina. Prior to appearing on *Drag Race*, Del Rio established herself as one of the most iconic drag performers in the US alongside other icons Linda Simpson, Lady Bunny, Sherry Vine and Hedda Lettuce. The latter three were featured alongside Bianca in the web series *Queens of Drag: NYC* in 2010 who also performed in the comedy special *One Night Stand Up: Dragtastic! NYC* on Logo TV.

After pressure from her peers and her own drive to "show 'em how it's done", Bianca Del Rio was cast in *RuPaul's Drag Race*. The immediate front runner and fan-favourite for her quick wit, strong performance in all aspects of the competition and "mama bear" disposition, Del Rio won three main challenges before taking out the crown of America's Next Drag Superstar.

The instant attention Bianca received following *Drag Race* enabled her film project *Hurricane Bianca* to get crowdfunded. The film is slated for a 2016 release and co-stars *Drag Race* alumni Joslyn Fox, Willam, Shangela and Adore Delano. Bianca continues to tour her comedy show *Rolodex of Hate* spreading her brand of poison-tongued hilarity across the world.

QUICK STATS

DRAG RACE:
Season 6

RANKING:
Winner

POST DRAG RACE:
Starred in the crowdfunded
comedy film *Hurricane Bianca*;
toured her comedy show
Rolodex of Hate internationally
from 2014 through to 2016;
performed at the 2015 Vienna
Life Ball alongside Courtney Act
and Eurovision's Conchita Wurst

SIGNATURE LOOK:
Old Hollywood Meets
Clown Realness

TYPE:
The Stand Up Comedian

FAN-FAVOURITE PERFORMANCE:
"Palladio" by Escala aka
"Bianca Del Rio Makes
a Dress on Stage"

Carmen Carrera

"If you find a flaw, let me know."

WHAT'S THE T?

Starting her drag career in the mid 2000s, New Jersey's Carmen Carrera started performing at legendary latino showgirl club Escuelita in the heart of Manhattan. Though many years prior to her transition into the beautiful transgender woman she is today, Carrera dealt with her sexuality and understanding of gender through honing her craft as a burlesque drag performer with the support of trans drag mother Angela Carrera. Improving her sex kitten act over the years, Carmen increased her bookings and went on to play The Polo Club in Hartford, meeting *Drag Race* alumni Manila Luzon and Sahara Davenport along the way.

Carrera was cast in the third season of *RuPaul's Drag Race* and although appearing as Christopher Roman out of drag, she became very well known for her perfect proportions and buxom booty, as critiqued by Jersey girl Michelle Visage as a crutch – "stop relying on that body!". Though wowing audiences with countless almost-nude runway presentations, Carmen – a member of the Heathers clique – didn't win any major challenges and was eliminated twice after being brought back by the judges for a second chance at the crown.

Carrera commenced her transition soon after taping *Drag Race* in 2010. Her flawless looks drew the eye of renowned fashion photographer Steven Meisel, who had Carmen star in his "Showgirl" *W* magazine and video shoot. Although touring her burlesque drag act less frequently, Carrera has become a trans role model starring, on occasion with television star Laverne Cox, in various reality programs addressing transphobia in the wider community.

QUICK STATS

DRAG RACE:
Season 3

RANKING:
6th place

POST DRAG RACE:
Featured on the fifth anniversary
cover of *C✱NDY* magazine
along with 13 other transgender
women including Laverne Cox
and Janet Mock; poster girl for
the 2014 Life Ball in Vienna shot
by David LaChapelle; Starred
in *Showgirl* – a Steven Meisel
W magazine shoot and promo
video; petitioned to serve as a
2013 Victoria's Secret Fashion
Show model

SIGNATURE LOOK:
Bulletproof Body Realness

TYPE:
The Jersey Showgirl

**FAN-FAVOURITE
PERFORMANCE:**
"I Am the Body Beautiful"
by Salt-N-Pepa

Chad Michaels

"Everything I've gone through has been because of Cher."

With over 20 years of experience as a drag performer Chad Michaels is the definition of an All Star and an icon – much like his own idol Cher. Drag daughter to the legendary Hunter, Michaels hails from San Diego and has performed as one of, if not *the* premiere, Cher impersonators in the world. Impersonation of the original diva has seen Chad entertain clubs across the US to Las Vegas stages and has given him the opportunity to perform for industry favourites such as Elton John, Christina Aguilera and Cher herself.

Entering the fourth season of the *Race* as a seasoned professional Chad Michaels was not only miles ahead of his competition in his understanding and execution of his drag skills but he set the bar for characterisation and polish. Although winning the "Snatch Game" as Cher and giving memorable performances throughout the season Chad finished as co-runner up with Phi Phi O'Hara. Chad's loss of the crown didn't last long as he was soon snatched up to compete in the first season of *All Stars* in which he took the crown and the first position in the RuPaul's Drag Race Hall of Fame.

Following his performance in both season four and *All Stars*, Chad Michaels continues to produce and perform in the *Dreamgirls Revue*, sharing the stage with, among others, his drag daughter Morgan McMichaels, Delta Work and Jasmine Masters. A master of impersonation Chad constantly reinvents his drag and his repertoire of characters with old school divas Bette Davis and new school icon Lady Gaga.

QUICK STATS

DRAG RACES:
Season 4 | *All Stars* Season 1

RANKINGS:
Co-runner Up | Winner

POST DRAG RACE:
Starred in CW's *Jane the Virgin*;
opened for Cher at the launch
of her "Woman's World" single;
Released single "Tragic Girl"
(2013) with Liquid360

SIGNATURE LOOK:
Polished Drag Mother Realness

TYPE:
The Drag Assassin

FAN-FAVOURITE PERFORMANCE:
"EOY (Entertainer of the Year)
2010 Medley" by Cher

Courtney Act

"If everyone else is relying on ugly, why can't I rely on pretty?"

WHAT'S THE T?

Emerging on Australian screens as both Shane Jenek and Courtney Act on the first season of *Australian Idol*, Courtney demonstrated her brand of fiery performance and camp sensibility enabling her to make it through to the Wild Card heat of the contest. Act immediately drew the attention of audiences, performing at the Sydney Opera House as part of the finale and touring Australia. Following the release of debut single "Rub Me Wrong" Courtney became a mainstay on morning television as a featured cosmetics spokesmodel. A big fish in a little pond, Act moved to the US in the early 2010s and became a West Hollywood karaoke hostess and YouTube star.

Courtney was cast in *Drag Race* and was soon seen as a contender for the crown. Despite a rocky reception from judge Michelle Visage accusing Act of "relying on pretty", Courtney delivered countless sickening runway presentations including her take on RuPaul in the iconic Bob Mackie silver gown. Building a friendship with on-screen star Chaz Bono as well as fellow contestants Darienne Lake, Adore Delano and Bianca Del Rio, Act came out as a co-runner up winning the adoration of new fans across the US.

After her appearance on *Drag Race*, Act became the first drag artist to perform with the San Francisco Symphony Orchestra in a performance with Cheyenne Jackson. Courtney continues to release music as a solo artist as well as with her American Apparel ad spokesmodel sisters Willam and Alaska, with whom she tours nationally and hosts a SiriusXM radio show.

QUICK STATS

Detox

"I am the queen bee so eat it up and crown it!"

WHAT'S THE T?

A long-time star of the WeHo drag scene, Detox – the alter ego of Matthew Sanderson – channels retro 80s style while opting for a performance style where this aesthetic is matched with a perfectly kitsch show sensibility. In her showtime staple "Nothing's Gonna Stop Us Now" by Starship, Detox marries Kim Cattrall's *Mannequin* with an outlandish 80s power suit and a frizzed weave for a perfectly camp power ballad performance. Prior to her appearance on *RuPaul's Drag Race*, Detox was a member of Californian band Tranzkuntinental alongside fellow *Drag Race* alumni Willam and Kelly Mantle.

In the lead up to her season of *Drag Race*, Detox was easily the most recognised personality to enter that race after a popular run of hit singles and music videos with her band DWV. Their 2013 single "Boy Is a Bottom" with over 20 million views, set the bar high for Detox who only won one main challenge in her run on the show. Showing her arse literally and figuratively on the main stage, Detox channelled her camp lip-synch style in all of her Lip-synch for Your Life performances including the iconic face off with Jinkx Monsoon to Yma Sumac's "Malambo No. 1". Her unexpected monochrome appearance at the Season 5 finale cemented Detox's status as one of the most stylish and fierce queens ever to compete in the *Race*.

An iconic and colourful drag artist, Detox currently tours internationally as a solo performer after the breakup of DWV and has slayed the MarcoMarco runway during Los Angeles Fashion Week for the last four years.

QUICK STATS

DRAG RACE:
Season 5

RANKING:
4th place

POST DRAG RACE:
Member of drag band DWV with
Willam and Vicky Vox; featured
model on Game Show Network's
Skin Wars; four-time runway
model for LA-based designer
MarcoMarco.

SIGNATURE LOOK:
Thierry Mugler meets
Jem and the Holograms Realness

TYPE:
The Style Icon

FAN-FAVOURITE PERFORMANCE:
"I Look to You"
by Whitney Houston

Ginger Minj

"I'm a crossdresser for Christ. I'll have you down on your knees..."

WHAT'S THE T?

Hailing from Leesburg, Florida, Joshua Eads-Brown has performed in the pageant circuit as Ginger Minj across the South for the best part of the 2010s earning her the titles of Miss Gay United States 2013 and Miss National Comedy Queen 2012. Inspired by Ginger, her favourite character on the 60s TV show *Gilligan's Island*, Minj had performed in the theatre since the age of four. A young queen in love with the classic funny ladies of yesteryear, she hosted *Broadway Brunch* in 2013 at Hamburger Mary's in Orlando; a full-scale musical production with a cast of fifteen with drag sister The Minx.

Following performances in the Orlando theatre scene in shows including *Chicago*, *Gypsy* and *The Wiz*, Ginger Minj competed in the seventh season of *Drag Race*. A plus-size queen and fan-favourite Ginger harnessed all her theatrical gusto to win the musical theatre challenge and give a memorable tribute to John Waters' "Pink Flamingos" in the parody "Eggs". Her strong performance in the competition pushed her to the final three where she came in as co-runner up with Pearl where she performed the original track "There Ain't No Way to Pray the Gay Away" as part of the reunion episode.

Following in the footsteps of *Drag Race* alumni Jinkx Monsoon, Ginger Minj has taken her powerful vocal ability, showgirl prowess and love for the classic era of cinema and created *Crossdresser for Christ* a confessional musical chronicling her own drag evolution and life story.

QUICK STATS

DRAG RACE:
Season 7

RANKING:
Co-runner Up

POST DRAG RACE:
Toured her musical comedy
Crossdresser for Christ in 2015;
performs "Christma-Hannu-
Kwanzaa-Ka" on the Christmas
album *Christmas Queens* (2015)

SIGNATURE LOOK:
Glamour Toad Realness

TYPE:
The Comedy Queen of the South

FAN-FAVOURITE PERFORMANCE:
"The Edge of Glory"
by Lady Gaga

Jinkx Monsoon

"I'm Seattle's youngest MILF."

WHAT'S THE T?

Performing in drag for the first time at 15, Jerick Hoffer began his on-stage career with performances at underage nightclub Escape and dance club The Streets in his hometown of Portland, Oregon. Following a move to Seattle Jinkx Monsoon emerged in a series of Funny or Die webisodes called *Monsoon Season*. A queen of all media and stage platforms, Jinkx continued her work in musical theatre with appearances in *Spring Awakening* and *Rent* as well as taking the title role in *Hedwig and the Angry Inch* in 2013. Prior to her appearance on *Drag Race* Jinkx became the subject of YouTube docu-series *Drag Becomes Him* exploring her life as Jerick and as Jinkx. This web series led to a film adaptation in 2015.

Inspired by the high concept characterisation of Season 4 winner Sharon Needles, Monsoon was inspired to audition and thus landed a position on the fifth season of *Drag Race*. A dark horse throughout, Jinkx was contantly pressured by fellow competitors and judges on the merits of her costuming and makeup skills. However, she perservered to prove that she didn't need to be the fishiest, most glamorous queen – she was a superstar in her own right. Not only winning the main challenges for the "Snatch Game" (in her iconic performance of Little Edie Beale) and "Drama Queens", Jinkx went on to take the crown over fan-favourite Alaska and pageant superstar Roxxxy Andrews.

Following her win, Jinkx worked on bringing her show *The Vaudevillians* to a wider audience. Through major performances of the show off-broadway and as part of Sydney Mardi Gras, Jinkx demonstrated that she is a different kind of winner to her predecessors – she's the drag Andrew Lloyd Webber!

QUICK STATS

DRAG RACE:
Season 5
....

RANKING:
Winner
....

POST DRAG RACE:
Toured her off-Broadway musical
comedy *The Vaudevillians*
internationally; released cabaret
albums *The Inevitable Album*
(2014) and *ReAnimated* (2015);
starred as the subject of
documentary film and web series
Drag Becomes Him (2015)
....

SIGNATURE LOOK:
Jewish MILF Realness
....

TYPE:
The Broadway Queen
....

FAN-FAVOURITE PERFORMANCE:
"Malambo No.1" by Yma Sumac
....

My goal is to always come from a place of

LOVE...

but sometimes you just have to break it down for a motherf**ker

Jujubee

"I like long walks on the beach, big dicks and fried chicken."

WHAT'S THE T?

Born from the drag scene of Boston, Massachusetts, Jujubee – the creation of Airline Inthyrath – was the creative fusion of her many years of studying theatre at the University of Massachusetts and her cultural upbringing as a Laotian American. Jujubee's aesthetic is often giving a cheeky nod to her Asian heritage while fusing traditional drag aesthetic and a slick street style.

A star from the second season of *Drag Race*, Jujubee won the hearts of the public despite never winning a main challenge. Her quick wit, warm disposition and cut-throat reading skills – "Miss Tyra, was your barbecue cancelled? Your grill is f*cked up!" – pushed the Laotian goddess through to the top three of the competition. Described as the first lady of lip-synch, Jujubee is one of the most iconic performers in the history of *RuPaul's Drag Race* and despite having been in the bottom two five times, never lost a single lip-synch. Her performances to "Black Velvet" by Alanah Myles and Robyn's "Dancing on My Own" (with Raven on *All Stars*) remain undisputed demonstrations of incomparable drag performance.

Following her season Jujubee has toured extensively both alone and with Raven with whom she shares the duo title "Rujubee" born from their appearance on the first season of *All Stars*. Her additional appearances as a mainstay professor on the spin-offs *Drag U* and *Drag My Dinner* with Manila Luzon and Raven has helped boost Jujubee's social media reach and has earned her a legion of fans on Facebook greater than any other Drag Racer.

QUICK STATS

Katya

"I'm just your average run-of-the-mill Russian bisexual transvestite hooker."

WHAT'S THE T?

Katya Zamolodchikova – everyone's favourite Russian doll – was born from the mind of Boston's Brian McCook. Inspired by the comedy genius of Amy Sedaris, Tracey Ullman and Maria Bamford, and Russian songstress Alla Pugacheva, Katya's humour is the perfect blend of random hilarity and Soviet sass. A high concept character like Tammie Brown or Sharon Needles, Katya sees herself as a "retired kindergarten teacher that becomes a street-walking psychic crime fighter who's also battling depression and schizophrenia".

One of the front runners from the get go, Katya served not only glamour but camp in her performances throughout *Drag Race*. An early Lip-synch for Your Life performance to Olivia Newton-John's "Twist of Fate" in a perfectly floral patterned air hostess outfit was enough fire under Katya to inspire very strong performances in the John Waters inspired "Divine Inspiration", "Ru Hollywood Stories" and "Prancing Queens" challenges. Although coming in fifth place Katya took out the title of Miss Congeniality for Season 7.

As her season aired Katya released simultaneous web series *RuGRETS*, a confessional detailing her regrets from each episode she starred in, and *RuFLECTIONS* a Russian-tinged poetic take on her character's eventful life. Since her season of *Drag Race* Katya has toured across the globe building her fan bases in Australia and in the UK.

QUICK STATS

DRAG RACE:
Season 7

RANKING:
5th place (Miss Congeniality)

POST DRAG RACE:
YouTube video vixen in *RuGRETS*
and *RuFLECTIONS* chronicling
her time on *Drag Race*; stars as
"Trish Thompson" in YouTube
web series *Irregardlessly Trish*;
Performs "12 Days of Christmas"
on the Christmas album
Christmas Queens (2015)

SIGNATURE LOOK:
Russian Bombshell Realness

TYPE:
The Cold War Comedy
Sweetheart

FAN-FAVOURITE PERFORMANCE:
"All That Jazz" (In Russian) from
Chicago (Original Soundtrack)

Laganja Estranja

"I'm too busy looking at my gorgeous body."

WHAT'S THE T?

A member of the legendary Haus of Edwards, Laganja Estranja (Jay Jackson) emerged from years working as a choreographer with Alyssa Edwards' Beyond Belief Dance Company in Dallas. Following a move to study in California, Laganja honed her drag talents alongside newcomer Adore Delano and went on to win a drag contest at Micky's in West Hollywood and subsequently a monthly guest spot alongside *Drag Race* alumni at the famed Showgirls drag night. A sickening dancer and performer Laganja quickly took the LA drag scene by storm with her dancing troupe Barbie's Addiction.

Although still a newcomer to drag, Laganja was cast in the sixth season of *RuPaul's Drag Race* following in the footsteps of drag mother Alyssa Edwards and sister Shangela. While a fan-favourite from the outset Laganja's performance through the season was green (pun intended) and lacked the experience of her competitors. Despite receiving a lot of tough love from the judges and Bianca Del Rio, Laganja went on to win one major challenge and finished eighth after two strong Lip-synchs against Gia Gunn and Joslyn Fox.

Determined to prove her star quality and exceptional dance skills Laganja has gone on to choreograph and perform alongside Miley Cyrus in the iconic 2015 MTV VMA performance, which starred over 30 drag performers. A star of World of Wonder's WOWPresents YouTube channel in shows *Alyssa's Secret* and *Bestie$ for Ca$h*, Laganja has also released her own solo single "Legs" and even developed her own marijuana-themed jewellery line.

QUICK STATS

DRAG RACE:
Season 6

RANKING:
8th place

POST DRAG RACE:
Tours internationally with the
Haus of Edwards alongside
drag family Alyssa Edwards and
Shangela; released single "Legs"
(2015) with rapper Rye Rye;
choreographed the Miley Cyrus
performance of "Dooo It!" 2015
MTV Video Music Awards

SIGNATURE LOOK:
Mary Jane Girl Realness

TYPE:
The Sickening Stoner

FAN-FAVOURITE PERFORMANCE:
"Beyoncé Medley" (with Barbie's
Addiction) by Beyoncé

Latrice Royale

"She is large and in charge. Chunky yet funky."

WHAT'S THE T?

Raised in Compton, California, Timothy Wilcots' drag persona Latrice Royale emerged in the mid 1990s at the Fort Lauderdale club The Copa where she won her first amateur drag contest. A natural performer with incredible work ethic and captivating moves, Latrice competed in the pageant circuit winning the title of Miss Pride South Florida in 2004.

Latrice Royale won the hearts of fans across the globe after her performance on the fourth season of *Drag Race*. By not only being a "B.I.T.C.H." (Being in Total Control of Herself) but also as a formidable costumier, performer and all-round polished queen, Latrice powered her way to the top four of the competition and won the title of Miss Congeniality. Lip-synch performances against Kenya Michaels ("You Make Me Feel Like a Natural Woman") and DiDa Ritz ("I've Got to Use My Imagination") demonstrated a world class style of classic drag artistry. In the months following, Latrice teamed up to form "Team Latrila" with Manila Luzon in the first season of *All Stars*, bringing back her timeless wit and warmth to the screen as a fan-favourite.

In the aftermath of her popularity on *Drag Race*, the now Florida-based Royale founded talent management firm All Starr Management, a 40-person strong team of talented drag acts, musicians and photographers including fellow Drag Racers Nina Flowers and Kennedy Davenport. Latrice has gone on to star in the Logo TV documentary *Gays in Prison* (2015) where she discussed her life behind bars prior to her appearance on *Drag Race*.

QUICK STATS

DRAG RACES:
Season 4 | *All Stars* Season 1

RANKINGS:
4th place (Miss Congeniality) |
7th place

POST DRAG RACE:
Introduced and performed
"You Make Me Feel (Mighty
Real)" with Jennifer Hudson at
Fashion Rocks; released dance
singles "Weight" (2014) and
"Thick Thighs (with Willam)"
(2015); officiates weddings and
civil ceremonies as a certified
marriage celebrant

SIGNATURE LOOK:
Diamante Diva Realness

TYPE:
The Large and in Charge Queen

FAN-FAVOURITE PERFORMANCE:
"Weight" (Season 7 Grand
Finale) by Latrice Royale

ALL SINS ARE FORGIVEN ONCE YOU START MAKING A LOT OF MONEY

Manila Luzon

"See – this is how you do drag girls!"

WHAT'S THE T?

After his first stint in drag as Cruella de Vil at 19, Karl Westerberg created similarly wigged beauty Manila Luzon in the late 2000s as he appeared in the New York night life as a club queen with partner and *Drag Race* legend Sahara Davenport. Demonstrating a strong eye for fashion with her conceptual couture from the outset Manila became a popular scene queen for her fun sense of costume construction and artistry.

Appearing in the third season of *Drag Race*, Luzon blitzed her way ahead of the competition in iconic couture ranging from Big Bird cosplay to pineapple ball gown realness to Louis Vuitton carrot-cake couture, some of which were created by later Drag Racer Ivy Winters. The winner of three main challenges and member of the feisty Heathers troupe consisting of Raja, Delta Work and Carmen Carrera, Luzon's strong work ethic and blend of glamour and camp pushed her to the top two of the contest, surrendering the crown to Raja. Her iconic performance of Donna Summer's "Macarthur Park" against Delta Work following the "Ru Ha Ha" challenge remains one of the strongest Lip-synch for Your Life performances in the herstory of the show.

In the years following Manila became one of the first queens to release her own music as well as starring as a playable character in the iPhone App drag game *Dragopolis*. Luzon's eye for fashion has also enabled her to collaborate with fashion designers Viktor Luna (from *Project Runway*) as well as walk catwalks for LA designer MarcoMarco on numerous occasions.

QUICK STATS

DRAG RACES:
Season 3 | *All Stars* Season 1

RANKINGS:
2nd place | 8th place

POST DRAG RACE:
Star of *RuPaul's Drag Race*
spin-offs *Drag U* and *Drag My
Dinner* with Raven and Jujubee;
released pop single "Hot
Couture" (2012) and dance track
"Helen Keller" (with Cazwell)
(2014); featured in television
advertisement "Red Ribbon
Runway" raising awareness
for HIV/AIDs

SIGNATURE LOOK:
Black and Blonde
Beauty Realness

TYPE:
The Filipino Fashionista

FAN-FAVOURITE PERFORMANCE:
"MacArthur Park"
by Donna Summer

Milk

"Milk! She does a body good, girl."

WHAT'S THE T?

In 2008 ex-competitive figure skater Daniel Donigan, inspired by his new boyfriend and friends' impromptu "10-minute-makeover" drag made his first ever drag transformation – a gender-f*ck "Little Merman" fusion of male and female attire with a killer heel. Addicted to online makeup tutorials Milk was soon born after a move to NYC where she was immediately snatched up by nightlife icon Susanne Bartsch – an old friend of RuPaul and the 90s club kids. Pumping out week after week of offbeat yet high-fashion looks, Milk and her drag posse the Dairy Queens took the New York drag scene by storm with their incomparable theme-oriented conceptual style of drag.

Milk's *Drag Race* audition tape was a rainbow wheel of innovative looks, comedic schtick and fresh creativity not seen before on the *Race* runway. Entering the workroom a statuesque flamenco-themed glamazon clown, Milk set the bar for her soon to be legendary looks which included her take on Pinocchio, Jon Benet Ramsey realness, RuPaul (the werkroom male Ru that is!) and the envelope-pushing bearded Gandalf moment in episode 1's runway. Expectedly punished by Michelle Visage's "When Will You Show Us Glamour" stick week in week out, Milk never succumbed to pressure to tame her creativity honouring her own sense of glamour and fabulousness until an untimely elimination in the sixth week of the competition.

Following *Drag Race*, Milk became a spokesmodel for the wacky and fun drag that had yet to be seen in six seasons of the *Race* and instantly won the following of both underground and bearded queens everywhere.

QUICK STATS

DRAG RACE:
Season 6

RANKING:
9th place

POST DRAG RACE:
Star of her own World of Wonder
produced web series *Milk's
LegenDAIRY Looks*; coverboy
for *Hello Mr.* magazine entitled
"Dan Donigan: Meet the Milk
Man"; runway model for the
2015 MarcoMarco LA Fashion
Week Show

SIGNATURE LOOK:
Club Kid Chameleon Realness

TYPE:
The Creative Clown

FAN-FAVOURITE PERFORMANCE:
"E.T. (Take Me Home)"
by Cash Cash

Nina Flowers

"LOCAAAAAAA!"

WHAT'S THE T?

Hailing from Bayamón, Puerto Rico, Jorge Flores Sanchez started doing drag at 19 against strong resistance from his family. Inspired by German punk rock artist Nina Hagen, Flores took her name and created Nina Flowers – an androgynous enigma that took the Denver drag scene by storm in 2008. Inherently creative like her Puerto Rican drag sisters back home, Flowers entered a drag scene populated by pageant queens and a pre-*Drag Race* world where the scene was not as established or welcoming as it is today.

Winning the online vote for the very first season of *RuPaul's Drag Race*, a then unknown TV competition loosely based on *America's Next Top Model*, Nina Flowers was from the outset a visually and conceptually different queen from pageant queens like Rebecca Glasscock, character impersonators like Shannel and dancing queens like Jade. Her honesty, warmth and heart were set against her strong and tattooed exterior making her such an original character that one could not only root for in the competition but adore her creativity and style. Finishing second to the first winner BeBe Zahara Benet, Nina took the title of Miss Congeniality and went back home to Denver where her drag was welcomed with open arms for the first time.

Following her appearances on *Drag Race* and *All Stars*, Nina has taken the club scene by storm. A star of the monthly Drag Nation in Denver, Nina continues to push boundaries with her style of Drag DJ'ing, releasing club singles and remixes, propelling her into the world of electronic music production. Nina is also lucky enough to have May 29 declared "Nina Flowers Day" in recognition of her contribution to Denver's LGBT community.

QUICK STATS

DRAG RACES:
Season 1 |
All Stars Season 1

RANKINGS:
2nd place (Miss Congeniality) |
9th place

POST DRAG RACE:
Spins internationally as one of
the most in-demand circuit DJs;
released house singles including
"Loca" (2009) and "I'm Feelin'
Flowers" (2011); starred in the
music video for Adore Delano's
"I Look Fuckin' Cool"
with Alaska

SIGNATURE LOOK:
All Star Androgyny Realness

TYPE:
The Genderf*ck Queen

FAN-FAVOURITE PERFORMANCE:
"Addicted to Bass" by Puretone

Pandora Boxx

"Anyone that's eaten my cherry pie raves about it."

WHAT'S THE T?

Inspired by fellow New York queen Darienne Lake, Pandora Boxx – the drag persona of Michael Steck – appeared on the Rochester drag scene in the mid-90s. Boxx, a classically styled female impersonator with a comedic flair, first appeared on US television screens in 1997 in an episode of *Ricki Lake* hilariously entitled "Get a grip doll...you're too fat to be a drag queen".

In 2009 Pandora Boxx was cast in the second season of *RuPaul's Drag Race*. Although her styling and aesthetic weren't to the taste of judge Santino Rice, Boxx won the hearts of fans through her camp schtick, killer impersonation of Carol Channing in the "Snatch Game" and through her honest discussion on suicide and depression. Crowned Miss Congeniality, Pandora went on to star in several spin-offs of *Drag Race* including *All Stars* and *Drag U*, as well as starring as the host of *Pandora Boxx's Drag Centre* – a web series where Boxx would recap newly released *Drag Race* episodes.

Following her season on *Drag Race* Pandora became the first well-known comedy queen of the franchise and went on to star in stand up comedy specials, which have starred future contestant Bianca Del Rio and drag comedy legends Coco Peru and Jackie Beat. Pandora has joined other *Race* alumni in releasing pop singles including "Cooter!" (2014) and "Different" (2015). Still touring strongly with the Battle of the Seasons Tour as well as appearing on all of the Drag Race Cruises, Boxx maintains her status as one of the original fan-favourites bringing her brand of camp and comedy across the globe.

QUICK STATS

DRAG RACES:
Season 2 | *All Stars* Season 1

RANKINGS:
2nd place (Miss Congeniality) |
11th place

POST DRAG RACE:
Writes for the Gay Voices section
of the *Huffington Post*; released
pop singles including "Nice Car
(Shame about Your Penis)" (2012)
and "Different" (2014); starred
in drag comedy series *She's
Living for This* in 2013; hosts
YouTube web series *The
Pandora Boxx Show*

SIGNATURE LOOK:
Colourful Comedienne Realness

TYPE:
The Susan Lucci of Drag

FAN-FAVOURITE PERFORMANCE:
"Let It Go" (Frozen Medley),
by Various Artists

Look at me —
a BIG OLD
BLACK MAN
under all of this makeup,
and if I can look
BEAUTIFUL
so can you

Pearl

"B*tch, I'm from New York and you can wear fur in spring. 'K?"

WHAT'S THE T?

Originally from St Petersburg, Florida, Matthew James Lent began his drag career in Chicago as Pearl in 2012. A feast for the eyes, Pearl creates performances and high-fashion looks that meld both Hollywood glamour and electric club kid aesthetics. Although a fairly new queen on the scene, Pearl has been lucky enough to curate her own eccentric queer club nights "Pleasure" and "Pain for Pleasure".

Pearl made her television debut on Season 7 of *RuPaul's Drag Race* in 2015. Executing intricately styled and aesthetically delicious looks on the main stage, Pearl was criticised for "falling asleep" throughout the competition. After the fire was lit under her by RuPaul for not making a splash like her fellow competitors, Pearl won two team-based main challenges with Max in a comedy hosting of the "DESPY Awards" and with Trixie as a "Conjoined Queen". Fighting off the early criticism, Pearl championed through to come as co-runner up with Ginger Minj.

Following *Drag Race* Pearl released her debut self-produced techno/dance album *Pleasure*, which featured the single "Love Slave" and charted at #11 on the US Billboard Dance/Electronic Album chart. In addition to releasing her own album, Pearl went on to team up with perfume company Xyrena to release Flazéda, her very own signature fragrance.

QUICK STATS

DRAG RACE:
Season 7

....

RANKING:
Co-runner Up

....

POST DRAG RACE:
Produced and released her own
dance/techno album Pleasure in
2015; curated her own signature
fragrance "Flazéda"; starred
in the music video to Violet
Chachki's single "Bettie"

....

SIGNATURE LOOK:
Stepford Wife Robot Realness

....

TYPE:
The Old Hollywood Club Kid

....

FAN-FAVOURITE PERFORMANCE:
"Hotride" by The Prodigy

Porkchop

"Victoria is very outgoing... she likes to meet men..."

WHAT'S THE T?

Beginning her drag career in 1987, Victoria "Porkchop" Parker was created from the mind of North Carolina's Victor Bowling. An astute and well-seasoned pageant queen, Porkchop has participated in over 200 pageants, won over 100 and taken four national titles including Miss Continental Plus in 2003. Inspired by Elizabeth Taylor, Porkchop's aesthetic is classic pageant drag, which has served her well for over two decades. Porkchop has starred in two documentaries on the pageantry system; *Trantasia* (2006) a documentary on The World's Most Beautiful Transexual Pageant and *Pageant* (2008) as a lead cast member vying for the title of Miss Gay America.

Cast in the first season of *RuPaul's Drag Race*, Porkchop holds the title of the first queen eliminated from the entire show, and as a result receives a warm welcome from RuPaul herself at all of the live reunion shows. Although an already polished and expert drag performer, it was Porkchop's weak sewing skills that brought about her early dismissal in the first challenge. Porkchop gave a show-stopping performance of RuPaul's "Supermodel" against Akashia in the first ever Lip-synch for Your Life of the series.

Porkchop has relentlessly toured since Season 1 concluded in 2009 and was lucky enough to be featured on stage with over 30 other drag queens at the 2015 MTV Video Music Awards for the Miley Cyrus performance. She is currently a member of Chad Michaels' *Dreamgirls Revue* based in California.

QUICK STATS

Raja

"I have a Master's degree in Fierce...I should be a professor!"

WHAT'S THE T?

LA's Sutan Amrull has performed as Raja Gemini for over 20 years as a self-described "glitter hippie, artist, performer, model and muse". Having dropped out of university, Raja decided early on that she had a flair for the artistic – painting, drawing and makeup artistry. Raja started drag in the early 1990s house music club scene where she created thrift store outfits and joined other punk club queens in the LA night life. Inspired by Leigh Bowery and rebelling against the sequins and shoulder pads, the edgy Raja was born and began not only her drag career but started working as a makeup artist. This artistry has formed the basis of Raja's career, which has seen her not only tour with Adam Lambert as his principal makeup artist, but saw her serve as makeup artist for nine cycles of Tyra Banks' *America's Next Top Model*.

Competing in *RuPaul's Drag Race* was a walk in the park for the likes of Raja – a seasoned performer with incomparable wit and sewing skills. Winning three main challenges and stealing the scene at every runway in looks ranging from African Zulu Realness to Rainbow Brite Cosplay, Raja easily took the crown beating fellow "Heather" Manila Luzon and Alexis Mateo in the final episode.

In the years following her win, Raja has released her own offbeat and edgy music videos and singles including the latino pop "Cholita" (2015) and Bollywood electro-disco "Zubi Zubi Zubi" (2013). Raja also now stars in the weekly web series *Fashion Photo RuView* with Raven with whom she was also a Drag Professor on the spin-off show *RuPaul's Drag U*.

QUICK STATS

DRAG RACE:
Season 3

···

RANKING:
Winner

···

POST DRAG RACE:
Toured the US as Iggy Azalea's
principal makeup artist; co-host
of World of Wonder's *Fashion
Photo RuView* with Raven;
released singles "Diamond
Crowned Queen" (2011), "Zubi
Zubi Zubi" (2013) and "Cholita"
(2015)

···

SIGNATURE LOOK:
Around The World In 80 Days
Realness

···

TYPE:
The Drag Chameleon

···

FAN-FAVOURITE PERFORMANCE:
"In My Arms" by Kylie Minogue

···

Raven

"I'm a man in a dress – I'm a psychological woman."

WHAT'S THE T?

After a stint as a male go-go dancer of the name Phoenix, David Petruschin from Riverside, California took flight and and emerged as Raven in the West Hollywood drag scene in 2002. Raven started her drag career alongside legendary sisters Morgan McMichaels and Mayhem Miller performing shows that suited her taste for the underground, stylish and electronic. A fan of non-mainstream artists like Fischerspooner, Róisín Murphy and Miss Kittin, Raven's performance style separated her from the pack as a dark horse.

Raven appeared on the second season of *RuPaul's Drag Race* and soon became a fan-favourite for her quick wit, icy yet fierce composure and striking aesthetic. Raven's style was equally matched with her makeup artistry, which saw her execute so many varied looks from baby blue blushing bride to *Cabaret*-era Liza and country sweetheart realness to disco-diva-meets-accomplished-author. Although incredibly determined and styled to the god, Raven was pipped at the post by both Tyra Sanchez in Season 2 and Chad Michaels in the first season of *All Stars*.

A lover of all things Disney, Raven continues to perform across the United States as one of the most fierce *Drag Race* alumni, often incorporating her love for the iconic cartoon house into her shows and aesthetic. Raven also now co-hosts the weekly web series *Fashion Photo RuView* with Season 3 winner Raja summoning her expert style, hair and makeup knowledge to "toot and boot" the looks of new *Drag Race* contestants on the runway.

QUICK STATS

DRAG RACES:
Season 2 | *All Stars* Season 1

RANKINGS:
2nd place | 2nd place

POST DRAG RACE:
Co-host of World of Wonder's
Fashion Photo RuView; music
video pin-up (MNDR's "Feed
Me Diamonds"); star of *RuPaul's
Drag Race* spin-offs *Drag U* and
Drag My Dinner with Jujubee
and Manila Luzon.

SIGNATURE LOOK:
Dark Temptress Realness

TYPE:
The Stone Cold Vixen

FAN-FAVOURITE PERFORMANCE:
"Megacolon" by Fischerspooner

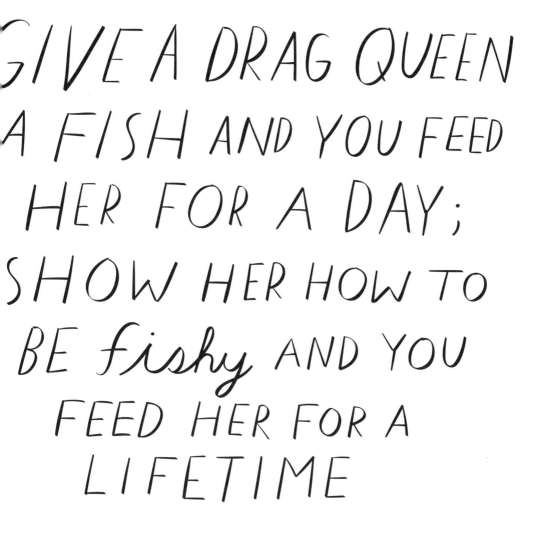

GIVE A DRAG QUEEN A FISH AND YOU FEED HER FOR A DAY; SHOW HER HOW TO BE *fishy* AND YOU FEED HER FOR A LIFETIME

Roxxxy Andrews

"I'm a pageant girl, big hair, big makeup."

WHAT'S THE T?

At 21 Michael Feliciano from Orlando made his first appearance in drag at a Halloween celebration and soon became the pageant beauty Roxxxy Andrews. Her namesake a fusion of Chicago's Roxy Hart and her drag mother, the legendary Erica Andrews, Roxxxy was inspired by the Orlando drag pageant. Drag sister of Detox, who also hails from Orlando, Roxxxy had taken numerous pageantry titles in her formative years including Miss West Virginia Continental Plus 2008–2009, the prestigious Miss Continental Plus 2010 and Miss West Virginia Continental 2012.

In 2013 Roxxxy Andrews was cast in *RuPaul's Drag Race* alongside drag sisters Detox and Alaska with whom the clique "Rolaskatox" was formed. A formidable contestant throughout, Roxxxy won the first costuming challenge as well as the "Super Troopers" makeover challenge. In an iconic Lip-synch for Your Life performance Roxxxy executed a wig reveal to Willow Smith's "Whip My Hair" that floored judges RuPaul and Michelle Visage who admitted, "I think I peed a little bit. Serious!". Finishing as a co-runner up with fan-favourite Alaska, Roxxxy Andrews fought heavy criticism from the public for her perceived bullying of winner Jinkx Monsoon.

Following *Drag Race* Roxxxy took on the role as principal makeup artist for Tamar Braxton (whom she impersonated in the "Snatch Game") on her US tour and walked the MarcoMarco runway. Roxxxy continues to perform across Florida as well as compete in the pageant system.

QUICK STATS

DRAG RACE:
Season 5

RANKING:
Co-runner Up

POST DRAG RACE:
Toured as Tamar Braxton's
principal makeup artist;
competed in 2015 Miss
Southernmost USofA Pageant
(1st Runner Up); runway model
for the 2014 MarcoMarco LA
Fashion Week Show

SIGNATURE LOOK:
Pageant Perfection Realness

TYPE:
The Thick 'N' Juicy Queen

**FAN-FAVOURITE
PERFORMANCE:**
"Talent Medley (at Miss
Southernmost USofA 2015)"
by Various Artists

Shangela

"Halleloo!"

WHAT'S THE T?

A comedian from Paris, Texas, DJ Pierce – better known as Shangela Laquifa Wadley – started performing drag professionally in 2009. She was only five months into her career in the LA drag scene before being cast in the second season of *RuPaul's Drag Race*. A member of the Haus of Edwards, Shangela cites *Drag Race* alumni Alyssa Edwards as her drag mother.

Although being eliminated first in Season 2 and subsequently winning the Entertainer of the Year 2010 pageant in Los Angeles, Shangela was re-cast in the third season of *Drag Race* where she finished in fifth place after a strong performance throughout the season. Shining in her characterisation of "Laquifa – the post-modern-pimp-ho" in the "Ru Ha Ha" comedy challenge, it was evident that while sewing wasn't necessarily her strong point, Shangela is one hell of a performer. The character of Laquifa went on to star on stage in her own comedy show as well as on *One Night Stand Up* on Logo TV. A fan-favourite *Drag Race* moment, Shangela's "out of the box" appearance in Season 3 was spoofed in Season 4 when Shangela announced she was cast in that competition.

A "werqin' gurl" through and through, Shangela has continued to deliver stand up comedy sets, including the Bianca Del Rio Roast for her 40th birthday. Teaming up with Lady Gaga and Courtney Act, the dancing diva starred in the lyric video of Gaga's "Applause" filmed at the famous Micky's in West Hollywood. Shangela has also been a busy queen on screen with appearances in TV shows *Dance Moms*, *Glee*, *2 Broke Girls* and *The Mentalist*.

QUICK STATS

Sharon Needles

"I'm a stupid genius, reviled sweetheart and PBR princess."

WHAT'S THE T?

Originally from Iowa, Sharon Needles moved to Pittsburgh in 2004 where she began working as a drag performer in nightclubs and later with the legendary experimental troupe the Haus of Haunt, which Needles described as "one punk rock, messy mash up of very talented, fucked up weirdos". It was here that Aaron Coady became the legendary Sharon Needles of today. The Pittsburgh collective included fellow *Drag Race* alumni, and later partner, Alaska, who shone through the season after Needles' debut.

In 2012 Needles appeared on the fourth season of *Drag Race* and quickly gained a dedicated fan base dying for her ghoulish, original style – in a season heavy with fishy, fashion-focused queens. Less an underdog than someone completely ignored among the breast-plates and sparkles, Needles repeatedly performed well – winning four of the challenges and only having to Lip-synch for Your Life once (where she battled it out with on-screen nemesis Phi Phi O'Hara). In the close-run finale, Needles snatched the crown from Chad Michaels to become The Next Drag Superstar.

Since *Drag Race*, Needles has busied herself releasing two self-funded albums *PG-13* (2013) and *Taxidermy* (2015). Sharon Needles has also become the face of PETA and regularly hosts horror and suspense B-Movies on Logo TV. Sharon continues to tour her live act as a part of the Battle of the Seasons tour alongside *Drag Race* alumni Ivy Winters, Detox and Phi Phi O'Hara.

QUICK STATS

DRAG RACE:
Season 4

RANKING:
Winner

POST DRAG RACE:
Released debut album *PG-13*
(2013) featuring singles "This
Club Is a Haunted House" and
"I Wish I Were Amanda Lepore";
spokesperson for People for the
Ethical Treatment of Animals
(PETA); was honoured by the
Pittsburgh City Council declaring
12 June 2012 the official "Sharon
Needles Day"

SIGNATURE LOOK:
Undead Goth Gurl Realness

TYPE:
The B-Movie Beauty

FAN-FAVOURITE PERFORMANCE:
"Sweet Transvestite" from
The Rocky Horror Picture Show
(Original Soundtrack)

Tammie Brown

"I don't see you out there walking children in nature."

WHAT'S THE T?

A drag icon of the Southern Californian scene, Tammie Brown – the creation of Keith Glen Schubert – got her start doing drag as a teenager in theatre productions of *Grease* and *Into the Woods*. Inspired by Tina Turner and Dustin Hoffman's *Tootsie*, Brown delivers an original blend of drag that recalls old Hollywood with an eccentric twist. Prior to her appearance on *Drag Race* Tammie pursued appeared on *The Surreal Life* and *How Clean Is Your House?*, and auditioned unsuccessfully for *America's Got Talent*.

Joining the first cast of *RuPaul's Drag Race*, Tammie was already one to stand out from the pack of nine queens vying for the title of the first ever America's Next Drag Superstar. Although her appearance lasted two episodes, Tammie – in true Brown fashion – vowed not to lip-synch for her life to Michelle Williams' "We Break the Dawn" against Akashia and simply smiled and danced back and forth into elimination. An iconic appearance at the Season 1 Reunion saw Brown go head to head with RuPaul and the judges on the merits of her drag and bullying from the judges – neither Ru nor Tammie were having a bar of it! The all-round zaniness of Tammie Brown won her a spot in the first season of *All Stars* where we were all "teleported to Mars".

After her *Drag Race* stints, Tammie Brown has continued to release offbeat folk and pop music including singles "Whatever", "Clam Happy", "Love Piñata" and "Walking Children in Nature" with long-time collaborator Michael Catti. Tammie continues her famous educational nature walks with city youth.

QUICK STATS

DRAG RACES:
Season 1 | *All Stars* Season 1

RANKINGS:
8th place | 10th place

POST DRAG RACE:
Released albums *Hot Skunkx* (2014), *Discos Undead* (2010) and *Popcorn* (2009); member of the band Rollz Royces with *Drag Race* alumni Kelly Mantle and long-time collaborator Michael Catti; starred in an advertisement for travel company Orbitz with fellow *All Stars* alumni Raven, Manila Luzon and Latrice Royale

SIGNATURE LOOK:
Yesteryear Glam Realness

TYPE:
The Countess of Kooky

FAN-FAVOURITE PERFORMANCE:
"What's Love Got to Do With It" by Tina Turner

When
you become the
image of your
IMAGINATION,
it's the most powerful
thing you could
ever do

Trixie Mattel

"I'm like the knock-knock joke of drag."

WHAT'S THE T?

Brian Firkus of Milwaukee, Wisconsin, began his drag career as Trixie Mattel, rebelling against the rough relationship he had with his stepfather — her namesake a reclaimed slur that Mattel would suffer at his hands. Though she won her first and only pageant there, Trixie was cut from a different yarn to many pageant queens, so a move to Chicago made for a fresh career challenge. It was here that she began working with Chicago club icon Kim Chi and perfected her now legendary overdrawn Barbie-inspired mug and curated the comedic drag act fans across the world have grown to love.

Cast in the seventh season of *RuPaul's Drag Race*, Trixie Mattel was an instant favourite for not only her original look but for her quick wit. Although shining in the "Glamazonian Airways" challenge, Trixie soon faced criticism for not standing out from the pack in her team's parody "Tan With U" and lost her Lip-synch for Your Life against Pearl. Following heavy criticism on social media for eliminating Trixie, RuPaul brought back all of the eliminated contestants in the "Conjoined Queens" challenge to earn a spot back in the competition. Teaming up with Pearl again as debutant twins, Trixie — the less-pretty twin — won her way back in the competition for another two episodes demonstrating both comedic and costuming skills that were lacking in earlier episodes.

Although she didn't make the top three, Mattel's star has continued to rise along with her fan base. Included is pop star Miley Cyrus, who has appeared wearing Trixie's official makeup-inspired sunglasses on Instagram.

QUICK STATS

DRAG RACE:
Season 7

RANKING:
6th place

POST DRAG RACE:
Presented a panel on makeup
at the first ever RuPaul's
DragCon convention alongside
Drag Race alumni Tatianna;
transformed the legendary
James St. James into a Trixie
clone on World of Wonder web
series *Transformations*; toured
Australia in 2015 with Katya

SIGNATURE LOOK:
Life-In-Plastic Realness

TYPE:
The Life-Size Doll

FAN-FAVOURITE PERFORMANCE:
"Barbie Girl" by Aqua

Tyra Sanchez

"I'm not a b*tch – I'm America's sweetheart."

WHAT'S THE T?

Florida's James Ross IV began his drag career after leaving high school at 16. Raised by her drag mother who brought her out of homelessness, Tyra Sanchez was taught in the trade of old-school Florida pageant drag and began impersonating Beyoncé in shows across the Orlando gay scene.

Looking to challenge herself and bring about a new life for her young son Jeremiah, Tyra was cast in the second season of *RuPaul's Drag Race*. Despite her youth, Tyra demonstrated a wide array of drag tricks and sickening stage looks. Winning three main challenges, Sanchez brought out her comedic side in the "Country Queens" challenge and was complimented by RuPaul for her old-school drag conduct in the "Here Comes the Bride" runway. Tyra's off-stage bridezilla drama with Tatianna provided iconic *Untucked* moments bringing the supplementary show to the forefront in its early inception. Never having to lip-synch for her life, Tyra Sanchez took the crown in a photo finish against Raven in a performance of RuPaul's "Jealous of My Boogie".

The youngest contestant to ever take the title of America's Next Drag Superstar, Tyra Sanchez went on to release her first single "Look at Me" in 2011 and work on a Kickstarter funded feature documentary by Björn Flóki called *Drag Dad*. Since taking the crown Tyra has been considered M.I.A from the *Drag Race* spotlight, which she revealed in a 2015 episode of web series *Hey Qween* was the result of her focusing on being the caretaker parent for her son Jeremiah in the formative years of his schooling.

QUICK STATS

DRAG RACE & RANKING:
Season 2 | Winner

POST DRAG RACE:
Became the subject of documentary film *Drag Dad* about her role as both a drag queen and father; starred as a fierce Drag Professor at *RuPaul's Drag U*; appeared as a Kim Zolciak doppelgänger on an episode of *The Real Housewives of Atlanta*

SIGNATURE LOOK:
Red Carpet Beyoncé Realness

TYPE:
The Seasoned Ingénue

FAN-FAVOURITE PERFORMANCE:
"Drunk in Love" by Beyoncé

Violet Chachki

"Pain is beauty and I'm the prettiest."

WHAT'S THE T?

Starting her career using a fake ID to gain entry into local Atlanta drag shows, Violet Chachki (Jason Dardo) was taken under the wing of drag mother DAXclamation! and soon became a regular cast member at nightclub Jungle. Working alongside drag royalty Amanda Lepore and Lady Bunny, Violet quickly cut her teeth and learned not only how to beat her face for the gods but learned burlesque show tricks like waist cinching and aerial silk performance. Chachki came into early notoriety for being photographed in the possession of Sharon Needles' official winner's crown after it was stolen during a 2012 gig in Atlanta – Chachki was later found innocent of the theft.

In 2015 Chachki was cast in *Drag Race* serving week after week of unmatchable runway looks. Winning the first main challenge, despite criticism from Michelle Visage for her un-cinched "boy body", Violet Chachki went on to win three main costume-based challenges. An expert in design and costume execution, her "I really could die bitch" 18-inch waist runway presentation floored the judges and fellow competitors. Chachki never fell into the bottom two and took the crown from Ginger Minj and Pearl in the live taped reunion finale. Much like young winner Tyra Sanchez, Chachki received heavy criticism for her cold and bitchy yet determined performance throughout the season.

Following her win on *Drag Race* Chachki has released her debut EP "Gagged" and attended the 2015 MTV Video Music Awards as Miley Cyrus' red carpet partner and on-stage dancer in the performance of "Dooo It!".

QUICK STATS

Willam

"I'm not gonna RuPaulogize for anything that I'm doing now."

WHAT'S THE T?

Willam Belli's drag career began at the same time as his acting career with appearances on The District, Boston Public and his starring role on Nip/Tuck as transexual Cherry Peck in the early 2000s. Supplementing his acting career with live performance, Willam formed the band Tranzkuntinental with fellow drag queens Detox, Vicky Vox, Kelly Mantle and Rhea Litré in 2009 before releasing his own solo parody "The Vagina Song" in 2012.

Cast in the fourth season of RuPaul's Drag Race, Willam was from the outset an accomplished screen queen with killer comedy chops to boot – a rule-breaker with impeccable style. Never forgetting to name-drop a co-star, designer shoe or ex-Sex and the City worn Dolce and Gabbana coat, Willam presented realness on the main stage and slayed the competition winning the "Float Your Boat" main challenge. Although a fan-favourite, Willam's time on Drag Race was short lived after a series of rules were broken in the now famous "What Did Willam Do?" shock elimination.

Willam can be credited as one of the hardest working Drag Race alumni with the release of two full-length albums and over 20 singles, hosting 19 episodes of Willam's Beatdown (plus 16 more self-funded and produced episodes of The Beatdown) as well as his now legendary spokesmodel work with American Apparel with Alaska and Courtney Act. Constantly working on parodies of popular music and currently working on his biography, Willam is showing no sign of slowing down.

QUICK STATS

Season 4 | 7th place

Performed as a member of viral drag troupe DWV as well as with the AAA Girls; released solo albums The Wreckoning (2012) and Shartistry In Motion (2015); Starred in TV's The New Normal (2013) and CSI (2012) and the film Kicking Zombie Ass for Jesus (2013); produces YouTube series Beatdown and Paint Me Bitch

SIGNATURE LOOK:
Whore Clown Realness

TYPE:
The Model Actress Mattress Whorespondent Ice Cream Man

FAN-FAVOURITE PERFORMANCE:
"Rich Girl" by Hall and Oates

If you can't love yourself how the hell are you gonna love somebody else?

Published in 2016 by Smith Street Books
Melbourne | Australia
smithstreetbooks.com

ISBN: 978-1-925418-05-7

CIP data is available from the National Library of Australia.

Publisher: Paul McNally
Design concept: Kate Barraclough
Design layout: Heather Menzies
Illustrator: Libby VanderPloeg

Printed & bound in China by C&C Offset Printing Co., Ltd.

Book 3
10 9 8 7 6 5 4 3 2